CONTENTS

INTRODUCTION 5

CHAPTER 1: OSTER DIGITAL OVEN BASICS 6

Oster Digital French Door Oven 6

Features of Oven 6

Control Buttons and Functions 7

Advantages of Oven 8

CHAPTER 2: BREAKFAST 10

Apple Oat Cups 10

Spinach Tomato Egg Muffins 11

Perfect Potato Casserole 12

Ham Cheese Casserole 13

Fluffy Breakfast Egg Muffins 14

Pumpkin Bread 15

Healthy Banana Bread 16

Baked Oatmeal 17

Healthy Oat Muffins 18

Baked Cinnamon Oatmeal 19

CHAPTER 3: POULTRY 20

Juicy Chicken Drumsticks 20

Crispy Chicken Wings 21

Lemon Pepper Chicken Wings 22

Delicious Turkey Cutlets 23

Turkey Spinach Patties 24

Turkey Meatballs 25

Healthy Chicken Fritters 26

Creamy Chicken 27

Easy Brown Sugar Chicken 28

Chicken Meatballs 29

CHAPTER 4: BEEF, PORK & LAMB 30

Beef Onion Bake 30

Simple Spiced Pork Chops 31

Quick Ranch Pork Chops 32

Pork Chops with Potatoes 33

Baked Pork Patties 34

Meatballs 35

Simple Lamb Patties 36

Baked Pork Ribs 37

Juicy Pork Tenderloin 38

Rosemary Pork Chops 39

Greek Lamb Patties 40

Lamb Meatballs 41

Pork Meatballs 42

Beef Zucchini Burger Patties 43

Smoked Paprika Pork Chops 44

CHAPTER 5: FISH & SEAFOOD **45**

Baked Salmon Patties 45

Simple Cajun Salmon 46

Tasty Crab Patties 47

Garlic Butter Shrimp 48

Sweet Dijon Salmon 49

Flavorful Shrimp Fajitas 50

Delicious Pesto Salmon 51

Garlic Tilapia 52

Flavors Catfish Fillets 53

Blackened Fish Fillets 54

CHAPTER 6: VEGETABLES & SIDE DISHES **55**

Parmesan Cauliflower Florets 55

Zucchini Tomato Bake 56

Zucchini Potato Gratin 57

Spinach Zucchini Casserole 58

Healthy Carrot Fries 59

Baked Curried Cauliflower Florets 60

Balsamic Mushrooms 61

Cheesy Broccoli Fritters 62

Creamy Broccoli Casserole 63

Baked Sweet Potatoes & Apple 64

CHAPTER 7: SNACKS & APPETIZERS **65**

Bacon Jalapeno Poppers 65

Perfect Crab Dip 66

Yummy Corn Dip 67

Garlic Cheese Dip 68

Baked Potato Wedges 69

Healthy Vegetable Bites 70

Tasty Roasted Chickpeas 71

Cheesy Cauliflower Tots 72

CHAPTER 8: DEHYDRATE **73**

Yellow Squash Chips 73

Eggplant Chips 74

Kiwi Chips 75

Kale Chips 76

Zucchini Chips 77

Banana Slices 78

Pear Slices 79

Salmon Jerky 80

CHAPTER 9: DESSERTS **81**

Delicious Pineapple Bars 81

Cinnamon Honey Pears 82

Cinnamon Apple Slices 83

Moist Yogurt Cake 84

Easy Blonde Brownie 85

Fudgy Chocolate Brownies 86

Soft & Moist Lemon Brownies 87

Easy Lemon Cookies 88

Chocolate Chip Cookies 89

CHAPTER 10: 30-DAY MEAL PLAN **90**

APPENDIX : RECIPES INDEX **92**

INTRODUCTION

The Oster Digital French door oven is one of the best innovative convection oven loaded with turbo convection technology which makes your daily cooking process faster. The Oster oven is perfect kitchen appliances capable to handle multiple tasks into single appliances. A digital touch control panel helps you to perform different cooking tasks like Bake, Broil, Toast, Warm, Pizza, Defrost, and Dehydrate. It looks attractive and stylish when you pull a single door to open both the door by just one hand pull. One of the best parts of the oven is it comes with extra-large interior space. The two rack position helps to maximize your cooking flexibility. So you can cook whole family food into a single cooking cycle.

The turbo convection baking technology is one of the innovative cooking functions added to the oven. Using this function you can bake your food faster and get even cooking and browning results. If you want to keep your food warm while you finish your work then use the warm function and set 6 hours. It is one of the best and economical ovens available in the market which consumes 50% less energy compare to other traditional ovens. It cooks your food faster but uses low heat to cook your food when you are using a convection setting. To reduce the mess the Oyster digital French door oven comes with a removable crumb tray. You can easily pull the tray for cleaning spills residues.

The Oster Digital French door oven cookbook contains 80 delicious and healthy recipes written from breakfast to desserts. All the recipes written in this cookbook are selected from globally inspired dishes and written into an easily understandable form. The recipes in this book are given with their perfect preparation and cooking time. Each and every recipe ends with their nutritional value information. This nutritional information will help you to keep track of daily intake of nutrients and calories. The book comes with a 30 days meal plan which helps you to plan your meal in advance. The advance meal plan saves your time and money. There are lots of cookbooks available in the market on this topic thanks for choosing this cookbook. I hope you love and enjoy the recipes written in this cookbook.

CHAPTER 1: OSTER DIGITAL OVEN BASICS

Oster Digital French Door Oven

The Oster Digital French door oven is one of the stylish looking convection oven designs to perform a multitasking purpose. It comes with a digital display which helps you to know about current running function, cooking time and temperature. It is also loaded with various one-touch functions like broil, bake, dehydrate pizza, defrost, warm, turbo convection, and toast. You never need to buy a separate appliance for a single function. The Oster Digital French door oven built-in high-quality stainless steel material that gives a compact and stylish look to your countertop oven. The digital control panel offers one-touch function keys which can make your daily cooking process easy and faster. You can easily open both the doors of the oven by just pull a single door by one hand.

The Oster Digital French door oven works on turbo convection baking technology which helps to cook your food faster and gives a nice brown texture over it. The turbo convection technology works the same as hot air circulation technology. It circulates hot air with the help of a convection fan which helps to distribute the heat faster and evenly around the food to give you even cooking results. The oven has an extra-large interior and comes with two rack positions so you can easily bake two 16-inch pizzas at once, roast whole chicken, and toast 14 slices of bread. You can set a maximum of 90 minutes for a single cooking cycle, after finishing cooking time the oven is automatically turn off. While using the dehydrates setting you can set a maximum of 6 hours of time. It consumes near about 50% less energy compared to a traditional oven. Due to the front glass door and interior light allows you to check the food without opening the door.

Features of Oven

The Oster countertop oven is loaded with various different features that execute your daily cooking tasks with ease and continence. These features are:

1.   **Removable Wire/Broil Rack**

The removable wire/broil rack is used when you are baking or broiling your favourite foods like burgers, sausages, chicken, and more. The space between the wire racks allows hot air circulation easily. It also helps to drain out excess fats and grease during the cooking process.

2.   **Baking Pan**

A baking pan is used to bake your food or you can use it under a wire rack while roasting or baking your food to avoid the spills and residues.

3.   **Interior Light**

The interior light of the oven allows you to see the cooking process during the cooking cycle without opening the door.

4.   **Digital Display**

The digital display helps to know about the functions you have to use the current cooking cycle. It also shows the remaining time and temperature during the cooking cycle.

5.   Internal Removable Crumb Tray

The crumb trays are used to collect the crumbs which are fallen down during the baking or broiling process. The crumb tray is easily removable from the oven for cleaning after finishing cooking.

Control Buttons and Functions

The Oster Digital French oven is loaded with various different functions and buttons that make your cooking process easy.

Bake: This function is used to bake your favorite cake, cookies, casseroles, muffins, and pastry. Oster oven circulates dry and hot air to bake your food quickly and evenly.

- First, select the proper position for the wire rack or baking tray.
- The rack position is mostly depending on food size and browning effect. If needed preheat the oven before starting the baking process. Place your food over a wire rack or baking tray.
- Select the baking function and adjust the desired time and temperature setting by pressing up and down arrow buttons.
- Press the start button to start the actual cooking process.
- The internal light turns on during the cooking cycle. When the cooking cycle completes light will turn off automatically.

Turbo Convection: This function is used with the combination of the bake function. It blows hot air with the help of a convection fan which gives you faster, even cooking results with a nice browning effect.

Broil: Using these settings you can broil pasta toppings, sandwiches, burgers, melting cheese spread, and more.

- Place your food over the broiling rack and set the rack in its right position then fix the baking pan under the broiling rack.
- Select the broil function. The display reads broil.
- Set desire broiling time from time setting by pushing up and down arrow buttons.
- Then finally press the Start button to start the cooking cycle.
- When the cooking cycle is in the process the internal light is on. When finishing the cooking cycle the light will off automatically.

Toast: This setting is used to toast your bread, waffles, muffins, and more.

- Place your food properly over the wire rack. Do not crowd food and set the wire rack into its right position.
- Select the toast function and set the shading by pressing up and down arrow keys.
- Press the start button. When the toasting is completed then open the oven door and remove the food from the oven carefully.

Pizza: This function is used to bake your favorite pizza. You can bake 16-inch size two pizzas at once cooking cycle.

- First set the wire rack to its desire position. Then place the pizza on the wire rack cantered position.
- Select the pizza function. The timer will show the default time of 20 minutes. You can increase or decrease the time settings as per recipe needs.
- The internal lights turn on during the cooking cycle. It turns off when the cooking cycle is completed.

Dehydrate: Using this function you can dehydrate your favorite veggies, meat, and fruits slices, and more.

- While dehydrating you cannot adjust the default temperature settings. Default temperature settings are set at 150°F.
- Select the dehydrate function and set the timer as per recipe needs. You can set a maximum of 6 hours of time.
- Then press the start button to start the program.

Defrosting: This function is used to defrosting fish and meats.

- Same like dehydrate here you cannot set temperature. The default temperature is set at 150°F.
- Select the defrosting settings and press time settings and press up/down arrow buttons to adjust the time settings between 15 to 20 minutes on each side.
- Then press the start button to start the cooking cycle.
- While the cooking cycle is running the internal light is on. When the cooking cycle is finished the internal oven light is off automatically.

Advantages of Oven

The Oster Digital French door countertop oven comes with various advantages some of them are as follows:

1. **Even Cooking Results**

The Oster convection oven has focused around to give you more even cooking results. It is equipped with turbo convection technology which ensures even and fast cooking results every time. The turbo convection technology works the same as the hot air circulation technique. It circulates even hot air around the food with the help of a convection fan into the cooking area to get faster and even cooking results.

2. **Saves your cooking time**

The Oster convection oven cooks your food by circulating hot air around the food with the help of a convection fan. The advantage of a convection fan is it cooks your food faster even at low temperatures. Compare to a traditional oven Oster oven takes a very short time to cook the food. It not only cook your food faster but also saves your electricity bill. Oster oven requires 50% less electricity compared to a traditional oven.

3. **Cooks More Food at Once**

The Oster oven comes with a large interior size having two rack position settings. This will help to hold a large quantity of food at a time. You can easily bake two 16 inch size pizzas at a time by placing it rack 1 and rack 2 positions respectively. The oven is also capable to hold whole chicken at a time and it also toasts 14 bread slice at once.

4.   Versatile cooking appliance

The Oster Digital French door oven is one of the versatile cooking appliances and capable to perform different cooking tasks like it Bake cakes, cookies, muffins, and more, Broils favorite burgers, toppings over pasta and more, Toast bread, Dehydrate meat, veggies, and fruit slices and make Pizza. To perform all these cooking tasks you never need to buy separate appliances.

FAQs

- **How many settings are given in the Oster oven?**

There are eight different settings options are given in the Oster oven. These settings include Bake, Toast, Broil, Turbo convection, pizza, warm, dehydrate, and defrost along with time and temperature settings.

- **Can I put tin foil over the wire rack while cooking?**

No, placing tin foil over a wire rack may overheat up the oven. It is not recommended to place the foil in the oven.

- **What is the turbo convection function?**

The Turbo convection function is used with the combination of bake function. It circulates hot air into the oven cooking chamber to cook food more even and fast.

- **Can I cook food on both the rack at the same time?**

Yes, you can place your food on both the rack position and you will get even cooking results on both the position at the same time.

- **Can I set the Dehydrate temperature manually?**

No, dehydrate setting temperature is set at 150°F by default. You cannot set it manually. You can only set the time period up to 6 hours while using this function.

- **Can I bake Pizza into Oster Oven?**

Yes, you can bake pizza in an Oster oven. The oven comes with has large interior space in which you can bake two 16 inch size pizzas at both the rack position at the same time.

CHAPTER 2: BREAKFAST

Apple Oat Cups

Preparation Time: 10 minutes
Cooking Time: 30 minutes
Serve: 12

Ingredients:

* 2 eggs
* 1 ¼ cups apples, peel & dice
* 2 tsp vanilla
* ½ cup applesauce
* 1 cup milk
* 2 tsp ground cinnamon
* 2 tsp baking powder
* 2 tbsp brown sugar
* 3 cups old-fashioned oats
* ¼ tsp salt

Directions:

1. Preheat the oven to 350 F.
2. Spray 12-cups muffin tin with cooking spray and set aside.
3. In a mixing bowl, mix oats, cinnamon, baking powder, brown sugar, and salt and set aside.
4. In large bowl, whisk eggs, vanilla, applesauce, and milk.
5. Add oat mixture into the egg mixture and stir until well combined.
6. Add apples and stir well.
7. Spoon mixture into the prepared muffin tin.
8. Place muffin tin onto the oven rack and bake for 30 minutes.
9. Serve and enjoy.

Nutritional Value (Amount per Serving):

* Calories 122
* Fat 2.5 g
* Carbohydrates 21.2 g
* Sugar 6.2 g
* Protein 4.3 g
* Cholesterol 29 mg

Spinach Tomato Egg Muffins

Preparation Time: 10 minutes

Cooking Time: 20 minutes

Serve: 12

Ingredients:

- 8 eggs
- 1/3 cup feta cheese, crumbled
- ¼ cup almond milk
- 3 basil leaves, chopped
- ½ onion, diced
- 1 cup spinach, chopped
- ½ cup sun-dried tomatoes, chopped
- Pepper
- Salt

Directions:

1. Preheat the oven to 350 F.
2. Spray 12-cups muffin tin with cooking spray and set aside.
3. Divide feta cheese, basil, onion, spinach, and tomatoes evenly into the muffin tin cups.
4. In a bowl, whisk eggs with milk, pepper, and salt.
5. Pour egg mixture over veggies.
6. Place muffin tin onto the oven rack and bake for 18-20 minutes.
7. Serve and enjoy.

Nutritional Value (Amount per Serving):

- Calories 68
- Fat 5 g
- Carbohydrates 1.5 g
- Sugar 1 g
- Protein 4.6 g
- Cholesterol 113 mg

Perfect Potato Casserole

Preparation Time: 10 minutes
Cooking Time: 35 minutes
Serve: 10

Ingredients:

- 7 eggs
- 8 oz cheddar cheese, grated
- 20 oz frozen hash browns, diced
- ½ cup almond milk
- 1 onion, chopped & sautéed
- 1 lb sausage, cooked
- Pepper
- Salt

Directions:

1. Preheat the oven to 350 F.
2. Spray casserole dish with cooking spray and set aside.
3. In mixing bowl, whisk eggs with milk, pepper, and salt.
4. Add remaining ingredients and mix well. Pour egg mixture into the prepared casserole dish.
5. Place the casserole dish onto the oven rack and bake for 35 minutes.
6. Serve and enjoy.

Nutritional Value (Amount per Serving):

- Calories 393
- Fat 27.8 g
- Carbohydrates 18.5 g
- Sugar 1.7 g
- Protein 17 g
- Cholesterol 147 mg

Ham Cheese Casserole

Preparation Time: 10 minutes
Cooking Time: 55 minutes
Serve: 12

Ingredients:

- 12 eggs
- 8 cups frozen hash browns
- 1 cup almond milk
- 8 oz cheddar cheese, shredded
- 16 oz ham, cubed
- ½ tsp pepper
- 1 tsp salt

Directions:

1. Preheat the oven to 350 F.
2. Spray a 9*13-inch baking dish with cooking spray and set aside.
3. In a bowl, mix cheese, ham, and frozen potatoes and pour into the prepared baking dish.
4. In a mixing bowl, whisk eggs with milk, pepper, and salt.
5. Pour egg mixture over cheese ham mixture.
6. Place baking dish onto the oven rack and bake for 55-60 minutes.
7. Serve and enjoy.

Nutritional Value (Amount per Serving):

- Calories 523
- Fat 31.7 g
- Carbohydrates 39.7 g
- Sugar 2.7 g
- Protein 20.1 g
- Cholesterol 205 mg

Fluffy Breakfast Egg Muffins

Preparation Time: 10 minutes

Cooking Time: 25 minutes

Serve: 12

Ingredients:

- 12 eggs
- ½ cup ham, diced
- ½ cup cheddar cheese, shredded
- ½ cup almond milk
- ¼ tsp garlic powder
- Pepper
- Salt

Directions:

1. Preheat the oven to 375 F.
2. Spray 12-cups muffin tin with cooking spray and set aside.
3. In a bowl, whisk eggs with milk, garlic powder, pepper, and salt.
4. Add ham and cheese and stir well.
5. Pour egg mixture into the prepared muffin tin.
6. Place muffin tin onto the oven rack and bake for 25 minutes.
7. Serve and enjoy.

Nutritional Value (Amount per Serving):

- Calories 114
- Fat 8.8 g
- Carbohydrates 1.2 g
- Sugar 0.7 g
- Protein 7.9 g
- Cholesterol 172 mg

Pumpkin Bread

Preparation Time: 10 minutes
Cooking Time: 35 minutes
Serve: 8

Ingredients:

- 2 eggs
- ¼ cup coconut flour
- ¼ cup flax seed meal
- ¼ cup Swerve
- 1 tsp baking powder
- 1 tsp pumpkin pie spice
- ¼ cup chocolate chips
- ½ cup pumpkin puree

Directions:

1. Preheat the oven to 350 F.
2. Grease loaf pan with and set aside.
3. Add all dry ingredients into the bowl and mix well. Set aside.
4. In a separate bowl, whisk pumpkin puree and eggs.
5. Pour wet ingredients mixture into the dry ingredients and mix until just combined.
6. Pour batter into the prepared loaf pan.
7. Place loaf pan onto the oven rack and bake for 35 minutes.
8. Slice and serve.

Nutritional Value (Amount per Serving):

- Calories 69
- Fat 3.8 g
- Carbohydrates 5.9 g
- Sugar 3.4 g
- Protein 2.6 g
- Cholesterol 42 mg

Healthy Banana Bread

Preparation Time: 10 minutes
Cooking Time: 55 minutes
Serve: 12

Ingredients:

- 2 eggs
- 3 ripe bananas
- 1 tsp baking soda
- 1 cup sugar
- 1 tsp vanilla
- 1 stick butter, melted
- 2 cups flour
- 1/4 tsp ground cinnamon
- 1/2 tsp salt

Directions:

1. Preheat the oven to 350 F.
2. Add bananas and melted butter in a mixing bowl and mash with a fork.
3. Add eggs and vanilla and stir until well combined.
4. In a separate bowl, mix flour, baking soda, cinnamon, salt, and sugar.
5. Add flour mixture to the banana mixture and mix until just combined.
6. Pour batter into the greased 9*5-inch loaf pan.
7. Place loaf pan onto the oven rack and bake for 45-55 minutes.
8. Slice and serve.

Nutritional Value (Amount per Serving):

- Calories 244
- Fat 8.7 g
- Carbohydrates 39.5 g
- Sugar 20.5 g
- Protein 3.5 g
- Cholesterol 48 mg

Baked Oatmeal

Preparation Time: 10 minutes
Cooking Time: 20 minutes
Serve: 6

Ingredients:

- 1 egg
- 2 cups old fashioned oats
- 1 1/2 tsp baking powder
- 1/4 cup maple syrup
- 1 1/2 cups almond milk
- 1 cup strawberries, sliced
- 1 cup blueberries
- 1/2 tsp salt

Directions:

1. Preheat the oven to 375 F.
2. In a bowl, mix oats, salt, and baking powder.
3. Add egg, vanilla, maple syrup, and almond milk and stir well.
4. Add strawberries and blueberries and stir well.
5. Pour mixture into the greased baking dish.
6. Place a baking dish onto the oven rack and bake for 20 minutes.
7. Serve and enjoy.

Nutritional Value (Amount per Serving):

- Calories 413
- Fat 18.7 g
- Carbohydrates 53.9 g
- Sugar 14.9 g
- Protein 9.3 g
- Cholesterol 27 mg

Healthy Oat Muffins

Preparation Time: 10 minutes
Cooking Time: 20 minutes
Serve: 12

Ingredients:

- 2 eggs
- 1 cup oats
- 1/2 cup plain yogurt
- 1/2 cup maple syrup
- 1 tbsp pumpkin pie spice
- 2 tsp baking powder
- 1 cup butternut squash puree
- 1 cup flour
- 1 tsp vanilla
- 1/3 cup olive oil
- 1/2 tsp sea salt

Directions:

1. Preheat the oven to 390 F.
2. Spray 12-cups muffin tray with cooking spray and set aside.
3. In a large bowl, whisk eggs with vanilla, oil, yogurt, butternut squash puree, and maple syrup.
4. In a separate bowl, mix flour, pumpkin pie spice, oats, oats, and salt.
5. Add flour mixture into the egg mixture and stir to combine.
6. Spoon the batter to the prepared muffin tray.
7. Place muffin tray onto the oven rack and bake for 20 minutes.
8. Serve and enjoy.

Nutritional Value (Amount per Serving):

- Calories 167
- Fat 7.1 g
- Carbohydrates 22.9 g
- Sugar 8.8 g
- Protein 3.5 g
- Cholesterol 28 mg

Baked Cinnamon Oatmeal

Preparation Time: 10 minutes

Cooking Time: 30 minutes

Serve: 8

Ingredients:

- 2 eggs
- 3 cups rolled oats
- 1 tsp ground cinnamon
- 1 tsp vanilla
- 1 1/2 tsp baking powder
- 1/4 cup butter, melted
- 1/2 cup maple syrup
- 1 1/2 cups almond milk
- Pinch of salt

Directions:

1. Preheat the oven to 350 F.
2. In a bowl, whisk eggs with almond milk, cinnamon, vanilla, baking powder, butter, maple syrup, and salt.
3. Add oats and mix well.
4. Pour mixture into the greased 8*8-inch baking pan.
5. Place the baking pan onto the oven rack and bake for 30 minutes.
6. Serve and enjoy.

Nutritional Value (Amount per Serving):

- Calories 341
- Fat 19.6 g
- Carbohydrates 37.3 g
- Sugar 13.7 g
- Protein 6.5 g
- Cholesterol 56 mg

CHAPTER 3: POULTRY

Juicy Chicken Drumsticks

Preparation Time: 10 minutes
Cooking Time: 45 minutes
Serve: 6

Ingredients:

- 6 chicken legs
- ¼ cup soy sauce
- 2 tbsp olive oil
- ½ tsp paprika
- ½ tsp oregano
- 1 ½ tsp onion powder
- 1 tsp garlic powder
- ½ tsp pepper
- ½ tsp salt

Directions:

1. Preheat the oven to 375 F.
2. Add chicken legs and remaining ingredients into the zip-lock bag, seal bag shake well and place in the refrigerator for 1 hour.
3. Place rack onto a baking tray then arrange marinated chicken legs onto the rack. Insert into the oven.
4. Bake for 45 minutes.
5. Serve and enjoy.

Nutritional Value (Amount per Serving):

- Calories 315
- Fat 20.1 g
- Carbohydrates 1.9 g
- Sugar 0.5 g
- Protein 30.5 g
- Cholesterol 105 mg

Crispy Chicken Wings

Preparation Time: 10 minutes
Cooking Time: 50 minutes
Serve: 6

Ingredients:

- 2 lbs chicken wings
- 1 tbsp baking powder
- 1 tsp Italian seasoning
- 1 tsp smoked paprika
- 1 tsp garlic powder
- ¼ tsp pepper
- 1 tsp salt

Directions:

1. Preheat the oven to 425 F.
2. Add chicken wings and remaining ingredients into the mixing bowl and toss well.
3. Place rack onto a baking tray then arrange chicken wings onto the rack. Insert into the oven.
4. Bake for 30 minutes.
5. Turn chicken wings and bake for 20 minutes more.
6. Serve and enjoy.

Nutritional Value (Amount per Serving):

- Calories 295
- Fat 11.5 g
- Carbohydrates 1.9 g
- Sugar 0.2 g
- Protein 43.9 g
- Cholesterol 135 mg

Lemon Pepper Chicken Wings

Preparation Time: 10 minutes
Cooking Time: 25 minutes
Serve: 6

Ingredients:

- 1 ½ lbs chicken wings
- 3 tbsp olive oil
- 2 tbsp honey
- ½ lemon juice
- ½ tsp pepper
- 6 tbsp butter, melted
- Pepper
- Salt

Directions:

1. Preheat the oven to 425 F.
2. Brush chicken wings with oil and season with pepper and salt.
3. Place rack onto a baking tray then arrange chicken wings onto the rack. Insert into the oven.
4. Bake for 25 minutes.
5. In a small bowl, mix honey, lemon juice, pepper, and butter.
6. Brush chicken wings with honey mixture and serve.

Nutritional Value (Amount per Serving):

- Calories 399
- Fat 26.9 g
- Carbohydrates 5.9 g
- Sugar 5.8 g
- Protein 33 g
- Cholesterol 131 mg

Delicious Turkey Cutlets

Preparation Time: 10 minutes

Cooking Time: 25 minutes

Serve: 4

Ingredients:

- 1 egg
- 1 ½ lbs turkey cutlets
- ½ tsp onion powder
- ¼ cup parmesan cheese, grated
- ½ cup breadcrumbs
- ½ tsp garlic powder
- ¼ tsp pepper
- ½ tsp salt

Directions:

1. Preheat the oven to 350 F.
2. Season turkey cutlets with pepper and salt.
3. In a small bowl, add egg and whisk well.
4. In a shallow dish, mix breadcrumbs, garlic powder, cheese, and onion powder.
5. Dip each cutlet in egg then coat with breadcrumb mixture.
6. Place coated cutlets onto the baking pan and bake in preheated oven for 25 minutes.
7. Serve and enjoy.

Nutritional Value (Amount per Serving):

- Calories 398
- Fat 12.6 g
- Carbohydrates 10.4 g
- Sugar 1.1 g
- Protein 56.1 g
- Cholesterol 177 mg

Turkey Spinach Patties

Preparation Time: 10 minutes
Cooking Time: 30 minutes
Serve: 4

Ingredients:

- 1 lb ground turkey
- ¼ cup breadcrumbs
- 4 oz mozzarella cheese, cubed
- ¼ cup parsley, chopped
- ¼ cup basil, chopped
- 2 tbsp Worcestershire sauce
- 1 tsp lemon zest
- 2 tbsp vinegar
- ½ onion, diced
- 1 tsp garlic, minced
- 1 cup spinach, sautéed
- 1 tbsp olive oil
- Pepper
- Salt

Directions:

1. Preheat the oven to 350 F.
2. Add all ingredients into the large bowl and mix until well combined.
3. Make four equal shapes of patties from the mixture and place onto the baking pan.
4. Bake in preheated oven for 30-35 minutes.
5. Serve and enjoy.

Nutritional Value (Amount per Serving):

- Calories 407
- Fat 24.9 g
- Carbohydrates 9.6 g
- Sugar 2.6 g
- Protein 40.5 g
- Cholesterol 131 mg

Turkey Meatballs

Preparation Time: 10 minutes
Cooking Time: 20 minutes
Serve: 6

Ingredients:

- 1 egg
- 1 lb ground turkey
- 2 tsp onion powder
- 2 tbsp ketchup
- ¼ cup parmesan cheese, grated
- ½ cup breadcrumbs
- 1 tsp garlic powder
- 1 medium zucchini, grated
- 3 medium carrots, peeled & grated
- Pepper
- Salt

Directions:

1. Preheat the oven to 350 F.
2. Add all ingredients into the large bowl and mix until well combined.
3. Make equal shape of balls from mixture and place onto the parchment-lined baking sheet.
4. Bake in preheated oven for 20 minutes.
5. Serve and enjoy.

Nutritional Value (Amount per Serving):

- Calories 221
- Fat 9.6 g
- Carbohydrates 12.9 g
- Sugar 4.2 g
- Protein 23.7 g
- Cholesterol 104 mg

Healthy Chicken Fritters

Preparation Time: 10 minutes

Cooking Time: 25 minutes

Serve: 4

Ingredients:

- 1 egg
- 1 lb ground chicken
- 1 ½ cups mozzarella cheese, shredded
- ¾ cup shallots, chopped
- 2 cups broccoli, cooked and chopped
- ¾ cup breadcrumbs
- 1 garlic clove, minced
- Pepper
- Salt

Directions:

1. Preheat the oven to 390 F.
2. Add all ingredients into the large bowl and mix until well combined.
3. Make small patties from the mixture and place onto the parchment-lined baking sheet.
4. Bake for 15 minutes. Flip and bake for 10 minutes more.
5. Serve and enjoy.

Nutritional Value (Amount per Serving):

- Calories 379
- Fat 12.6 g
- Carbohydrates 23.4 g
- Sugar 2.1 g
- Protein 42 g
- Cholesterol 147 mg

Creamy Chicken

Preparation Time: 10 minutes
Cooking Time: 55 minutes
Serve: 4

Ingredients:

- 4 chicken breasts
- 1 tsp garlic powder
- 1 tsp dried basil
- 1 tsp dried oregano
- ¾ cup parmesan cheese, grated
- 1 cup sour cream
- 1 cup mozzarella cheese, shredded
- Pepper
- Salt

Directions:

1. Preheat the oven to 375 F.
2. Spray casserole dish with cooking spray and set aside.
3. Place chicken breasts into the prepared casserole dish and top with mozzarella cheese.
4. In a bowl, mix sour cream, parmesan cheese, oregano, basil, garlic powder, pepper, and salt.
5. Pour sour cream mixture over chicken breasts.
6. Place casserole dish onto the oven rack and bake for 55-60 minutes.
7. Serve and enjoy.

Nutritional Value (Amount per Serving):

- Calories 574
- Fat 33.2 g
- Carbohydrates 3.5 g
- Sugar 0.3 g
- Protein 58.3 g
- Cholesterol 189 mg

Easy Brown Sugar Chicken

Preparation Time: 10 minutes

Cooking Time: 30 minutes

Serve: 4

Ingredients:

- 4 chicken breasts, boneless & skinless
- ¼ cup brown sugar
- 1 tbsp garlic, minced & sautéed
- Pepper
- Salt

Directions:

1. Preheat the oven to 450 F.
2. Spray casserole dish with cooking spray and set aside.
3. Season chicken breasts with pepper and salt and place into the casserole dish.
4. Mix together brown sugar and garlic and sprinkle over chicken.
5. Place casserole dish onto the oven rack and bake for 25-30 minutes.
6. Serve and enjoy.

Nutritional Value (Amount per Serving):

- Calories 345
- Fat 14.3 g
- Carbohydrates 9.6 g
- Sugar 8.8 g
- Protein 42.4 g
- Cholesterol 130 mg

Chicken Meatballs

Preparation Time: 10 minutes
Cooking Time: 25 minutes
Serve: 6

Ingredients:

- 1 egg
- 1 lb ground chicken
- ¼ cup fresh parsley, chopped
- ½ tsp dried oregano
- ½ tsp garlic powder
- ½ cup parmesan cheese, grated
- ½ cup breadcrumbs
- ½ tsp onion powder
- 1 tsp pepper
- ½ tsp salt

Directions:

1. Preheat the oven to 400 F.
2. Add all ingredients into the mixing bowl and mix until well combined.
3. Make equal shape of balls from meat mixture and place onto the parchment-lined baking sheet.
4. Bake in preheated oven for 25-30 minutes.
5. Serve and enjoy.

Nutritional Value (Amount per Serving):

- Calories 193
- Fat 6.9 g
- Carbohydrates 7.3 g
- Sugar 0.8 g
- Protein 24.2 g
- Cholesterol 95 mg

CHAPTER 4: BEEF, PORK & LAMB

Beef Onion Bake

Preparation Time: 10 minutes
Cooking Time: 30 minutes
Serve: 6

Ingredients:

- 1 lb ground beef
- 2 cups fried onions
- 2 cups cheddar cheese, shredded
- 1 tsp Worcestershire sauce
- 1 tsp garlic powder
- 16 oz French onion dip
- 10.5 oz cream of mushrooms soup
- 10 oz pasta, uncooked

Directions:

1. Preheat the oven to 350 F.
2. Cook pasta according to the packet instructions and drain well.
3. Brown the meat with Worcestershire sauce and garlic powder over medium heat. Drain meat.
4. Add onion dip and cream of mushroom soup into the browned meat and simmer for 5 minutes over low heat.
5. Add pasta to the meat mixture and mix well. Pour meat mixture into the greased 9*13-inch casserole dish and top with cheddar cheese and fried onions.
6. Place casserole dish onto the oven rack and bake for 20-25 minutes.
7. Serve and enjoy.

Nutritional Value (Amount per Serving):

- Calories 742
- Fat 44.5 g
- Carbohydrates 43 g
- Sugar 3.3 g
- Protein 40.9 g
- Cholesterol 193 mg

Simple Spiced Pork Chops

Preparation Time: 10 minutes
Cooking Time: 20 minutes
Serve: 4

Ingredients:

- 4 pork chops, boneless
- 2 tbsp olive oil
- For the dry rub:
- ¼ tsp pepper
- ½ tsp Italian seasoning
- ½ tsp garlic powder
- 2 tbsp brown sugar
- 1 tsp smoked paprika
- ½ tsp sea salt

Directions:

1. Preheat the oven to 375 F.
2. Brush pork chops with olive oil.
3. In a small bowl, mix together all rub ingredients and rub all over pork chops.
4. Place pork chops onto the baking pan and bake in preheated oven for 20-25 minutes.
5. Serve and enjoy.

Nutritional Value (Amount per Serving):

- Calories 338
- Fat 27.1 g
- Carbohydrates 5.1 g
- Sugar 4.6 g
- Protein 18.1 g
- Cholesterol 69 mg

Quick Ranch Pork Chops

Preparation Time: 10 minutes

Cooking Time: 30 minutes

Serve: 6

Ingredients:

- 6 pork chops, boneless
- 1 tsp dried parsley
- 2 tbsp dry ranch mix
- 4 tbsp olive oil

Directions:

1. Preheat the oven to 425 F.
2. Place pork chops into the baking dish.
3. Mix oil, dry ranch mix, and parsley and spoon over pork chops.
4. Place baking dish onto the oven rack and bake for 30 minutes.
5. Serve and enjoy.

Nutritional Value (Amount per Serving):

- Calories 336
- Fat 29.2 g
- Carbohydrates 0 g
- Sugar 0 g
- Protein 18 g
- Cholesterol 69 mg

Pork Chops with Potatoes

Preparation Time: 10 minutes

Cooking Time: 20 minutes

Serve: 6

Ingredients:

- 6 pork chops, bone-in
- 1 oz dried Italian dressing mix
- ¼ cup olive oil
- 1 onion, chopped
- 1 lb baby potatoes, quartered
- Pepper
- Salt

Directions:

1. Preheat the oven to 425 F.
2. Arrange pork chops, onions, and potatoes onto the greased baking pan.
3. In a small bowl, mix oil, Italian dressing mix, pepper, and salt, and spoon over pork chops.
4. Place the baking pan onto the oven rack and bake for 15-20 minutes.
5. Serve and enjoy.

Nutritional Value (Amount per Serving):

- Calories 393
- Fat 28.5 g
- Carbohydrates 14.1 g
- Sugar 0.8 g
- Protein 20.3 g
- Cholesterol 69 mg

Baked Pork Patties

Preparation Time: 10 minutes
Cooking Time: 30 minutes
Serve: 6

Ingredients:

- 1 egg
- 2 ¼ lbs ground pork
- ½ cup breadcrumbs
- 1 tsp garlic powder
- 1 tsp paprika
- 1 onion, minced
- 1 carrot, minced
- ½ tsp pepper
- 1 tsp salt

Directions:

1. Preheat the oven to 375 F.
2. Add all ingredients into the mixing bowl and mix until well combined.
3. Make six equal shapes of patties from mixture and place onto the greased baking pan and bake in preheated oven for 25-35 minutes.
4. Serve and enjoy.

Nutritional Value (Amount per Serving):

- Calories 304
- Fat 7.3 g
- Carbohydrates 9.9 g
- Sugar 2.1 g
- Protein 47.1 g
- Cholesterol 151 mg

Meatballs

Preparation Time: 10 minutes

Cooking Time: 20 minutes

Serve: 4

Ingredients:

- 1 lb ground lamb
- ¼ tsp dried basil
- ¼ tsp dried oregano
- 1 garlic clove, minced
- ¼ cup fresh cilantro, chopped
- ¼ cup raisins
- ¼ cup yogurt
- 2 bread slices, cut into small pieces
- Pepper
- Salt

Directions:

1. Preheat the oven to 375 F.
2. Add all ingredients into the mixing bowl and mix until well combined.
3. Make equal shape of balls from meat mixture and place onto the parchment-lined baking pan.
4. Bake for 20 minutes.
5. Serve and enjoy.

Nutritional Value (Amount per Serving):

- Calories 263
- Fat 8.7 g
- Carbohydrates 10.9 g
- Sugar 6.7 g
- Protein 33.4 g
- Cholesterol 103 mg

Simple Lamb Patties

Preparation Time: 10 minutes

Cooking Time: 20 minutes

Serve: 6

Ingredients:

- 1 ½ lbs ground lamb
- 1 tbsp fresh ginger, grated
- 3 green onions, sliced
- Pepper
- Salt

Directions:

1. Preheat the oven to 375 F.
2. Add all ingredients into the mixing bowl and mix until well combined.
3. Make six equal shapes of patties from meat mixture and place onto the parchment-lined baking pan.
4. Bake for 20 minutes.
5. Serve and enjoy.

Nutritional Value (Amount per Serving):

- Calories 216
- Fat 8.4 g
- Carbohydrates 1.2 g
- Sugar 0.2 g
- Protein 32.1 g
- Cholesterol 102 mg

Baked Pork Ribs

Preparation Time: 10 minutes
Cooking Time: 30 minutes
Serve: 8

Ingredients:

- 2 lbs pork ribs, boneless
- 1 tbsp onion powder
- 1 ½ tbsp garlic powder
- ½ tsp Italian seasoning
- 2 tbsp olive oil
- Pepper
- Salt

Directions:

1. Preheat the oven to 350 F.
2. In a small bowl, mix onion powder, garlic powder, Italian seasoning, pepper, and salt.
3. Brush pork ribs with oil and rub with spices mixture.
4. Place pork ribs onto the baking pan and bake for 25-30 minutes.
5. Serve and enjoy.

Nutritional Value (Amount per Serving):

- Calories 319
- Fat 20.2 g
- Carbohydrates 1.9 g
- Sugar 0.7 g
- Protein 30.4 g
- Cholesterol 117 mg

Juicy Pork Tenderloin

Preparation Time: 10 minutes
Cooking Time: 20 minutes
Serve: 6

Ingredients:

- 2 lbs pork tenderloin
- ¼ cup honey
- ¼ cup soy sauce
- 1 tbsp garlic, minced
- 1 tsp dried oregano
- 1 tbsp olive oil
- Pepper
- Salt

Directions:

1. Preheat the oven to 350 F.
2. Add honey and soy sauce into the small saucepan and cook until reduced by half.
3. Mix garlic, oregano, pepper, and salt and rub all over pork tenderloin.
4. Heat oil in a large pan over medium heat. Cook tenderloin on each side for 2 minutes.
5. Place pork tenderloin onto the baking sheet and baste with honey mixture.
6. Bake in preheated oven for 20 minutes.
7. Slice and serve.

Nutritional Value (Amount per Serving):

- Calories 288
- Fat 7.7 g
- Carbohydrates 13.1 g
- Sugar 11.8 g
- Protein 40.4 g
- Cholesterol 110 mg

Rosemary Pork Chops

Preparation Time: 10 minutes

Cooking Time: 25 minutes

Serve: 4

Ingredients:

- 4 pork chops, boneless and cut 1/2-inch thick
- 1 tsp dried rosemary, crushed
- 1 tbsp olive oil
- 1/4 tsp pepper
- 1/4 tsp salt

Directions:

1. Preheat the oven to 350 F.
2. Season pork chops with pepper and salt.
3. Mix rosemary and oil and rub all over pork chops.
4. Place pork chops onto the baking pan and bake for 25 minutes.
5. Serve and enjoy.

Nutritional Value (Amount per Serving):

- Calories 257
- Fat 19.9 g
- Carbohydrates 0.3 g
- Sugar 0 g
- Protein 18 g
- Cholesterol 69 mg

Greek Lamb Patties

Preparation Time: 10 minutes

Cooking Time: 8 minutes

Serve: 4

Ingredients:

- 1 lb ground lamb
- 1 cup feta cheese, crumbled
- 1 tbsp garlic, minced
- 1 jalapeno pepper, minced
- 4 basil leaves, minced
- 10 mint leaves, minced
- 1/4 cup fresh parsley, chopped
- 1 tsp dried oregano
- 1/4 tsp pepper
- 1/2 tsp kosher salt

Directions:

1. Preheat the oven to 390 F.
2. All ingredients into the mixing bowl and mix until well combined.
3. Make four equal shapes of patties and place them onto the baking pan.
4. Bake for 8 minutes.
5. Serve and enjoy.

Nutritional Value (Amount per Serving):

- Calories 317
- Fat 16.4 g
- Carbohydrates 3 g
- Sugar 1.7 g
- Protein 37.5 g
- Cholesterol 135 mg

Lamb Meatballs

Preparation Time: 10 minutes
Cooking Time: 20 minutes
Serve: 4

Ingredients:

- 1 egg, lightly beaten
- 1 lb ground lamb
- 2 tsp fresh oregano, chopped
- 2 tbsp fresh parsley, chopped
- 1 tbsp garlic, minced
- 1/4 tsp pepper
- 1/4 tsp red pepper flakes
- 1 tsp ground cumin
- 1 tsp kosher salt

Directions:

1. Preheat the oven to 425 F.
2. Add all ingredients into the mixing bowl and mix until well combined.
3. Make small balls from the meat mixture and place onto baking sheet.
4. Bake for 20 minutes.
5. Serve and enjoy.

Nutritional Value (Amount per Serving):

- Calories 325
- Fat 20.2 g
- Carbohydrates 1.7 g
- Sugar 0.2 g
- Protein 33.6 g
- Cholesterol 143 mg

Pork Meatballs

Preparation Time: 10 minutes
Cooking Time: 15 minutes
Serve: 4

Ingredients:

- 1 lb ground pork
- 1 tsp smoked paprika
- 1 tsp garlic powder
- 1 tsp onion powder
- 1/2 tsp ground cumin
- 1/2 tsp coriander
- 1/2 tsp dried thyme
- Pepper
- Salt

Directions:

1. Preheat the oven to 400 F.
2. Add all ingredients into the large bowl and mix until well combined.
3. Make small balls from the meat mixture and place onto the baking sheet.
4. Bake for 15 minutes.
5. Serve and enjoy.

Nutritional Value (Amount per Serving):

- Calories 170
- Fat 4.1 g
- Carbohydrates 1.5 g
- Sugar 0.4 g
- Protein 30 g
- Cholesterol 83 mg

Beef Zucchini Burger Patties

Preparation Time: 10 minutes
Cooking Time: 35 minutes
Serve: 6

Ingredients:

- 1 lb ground beef
- 2 eggs, lightly beaten
- 1/2 onion, chopped
- 2 medium zucchini, grated and squeeze out all liquid
- 1/2 tsp chili powder
- 1 tsp curry powder
- 1 cup breadcrumbs
- Pepper
- Salt

Directions:

1. Preheat the oven to 400 F.
2. Add all ingredients into the large bowl and mix until well combined.
3. Make six equal shapes patties from meat mixture and place onto baking sheet.
4. Bake for 35 minutes.
5. Serve and enjoy.

Nutritional Value (Amount per Serving):

- Calories 248
- Fat 7.3 g
- Carbohydrates 16.4 g
- Sugar 2.8 g
- Protein 28.1 g
- Cholesterol 122 mg

Smoked Paprika Pork Chops

Preparation Time: 10 minutes

Cooking Time: 25 minutes

Serve: 2

Ingredients:

- 2 pork chops
- 2 tsp brown sugar
- 1 tsp smoked paprika
- Pepper
- Salt

Directions:

1. Preheat the oven to 325 F.
2. Mix smoked paprika, brown sugar, pepper, and salt and rub all over pork chops.
3. Place pork chops into the baking dish.
4. Bake for 25 minutes.
5. Serve and enjoy.

Nutritional Value (Amount per Serving):

- Calories 271
- Fat 20 g
- Carbohydrates 3.6 g
- Sugar 3 g
- Protein 18.1 g
- Cholesterol 69 mg

CHAPTER 5: FISH & SEAFOOD

Baked Salmon Patties

Preparation Time: 10 minutes
Cooking Time: 20 minutes
Serve: 4

Ingredients:

- 2 eggs, lightly beaten
- 14 oz can salmon, drained and flaked with a fork
- 1/4 cup breadcrumbs
- 1 tbsp garlic, minced
- 1/2 cup fresh parsley, chopped
- 1 tsp Dijon mustard
- Pepper
- Salt

Directions:

1. Preheat the oven to 400 F.
2. Add all ingredients into the large bowl and mix until well combined.
3. Make four equal shapes of patties from the mixture and place onto the baking sheet.
4. Bake for 10 minutes.
5. Flip patties and bake for 10 minutes more.
6. Serve and enjoy.

Nutritional Value (Amount per Serving):

- Calories 203
- Fat 8.7 g
- Carbohydrates 6.3 g
- Sugar 0.7 g
- Protein 23.7 g
- Cholesterol 136 mg

Simple Cajun Salmon

Preparation Time: 10 minutes
Cooking Time: 12 minutes
Serve: 4

Ingredients:

- 4 salmon fillets
- 1 ½ tsp Cajun seasoning
- ¼ cup brown sugar
- Pepper
- Salt

Directions:

1. Preheat the oven to 400 F.
2. Mix brown sugar, Cajun seasoning, pepper, and salt and rub all over salmon fillets.
3. Place salmon fillets onto the baking pan and bake for 12 minutes.
4. Serve and enjoy.

Nutritional Value (Amount per Serving):

- Calories 270
- Fat 10 g
- Carbohydrates 8 g
- Sugar 8 g
- Protein 34 g
- Cholesterol 75 mg

Tasty Crab Patties

Preparation Time: 10 minutes
Cooking Time: 30 minutes
Serve: 6

Ingredients:

- 15 oz lump crab meat
- 1/4 cup celery, diced
- 1/4 cup onion, diced
- 1 cup crushed crackers
- 1 tsp old bay seasoning
- 1 tsp mustard
- 2/3 cup mashed avocado

Directions:

1. Preheat the oven to 350 F.
2. Add all ingredients into the mixing bowl and mix until just combined.
3. Make six equal shapes of patties from the mixture and place onto the baking sheet.
4. Bake for 30 minutes.
5. Serve and enjoy.

Nutritional Value (Amount per Serving):

- Calories 155
- Fat 12 g
- Carbohydrates 12 g
- Sugar 2 g
- Protein 12 g
- Cholesterol 42 mg

Garlic Butter Shrimp

Preparation Time: 10 minutes
Cooking Time: 15 minutes
Serve: 4

Ingredients:

- 1 lb shrimp, peel & deveined
- 4 garlic cloves, pressed
- 2 tbsp butter, melted
- 2 tbsp fresh lemon juice

Directions:

1. Preheat the oven to 375 F.
2. Add shrimp, garlic, butter, and lemon juice into the mixing bowl and toss well.
3. Pour shrimp into the baking pan.
4. Place the baking pan onto the oven rack and bake for 15 minutes.
5. Serve and enjoy.

Nutritional Value (Amount per Serving):

- Calories 196
- Fat 7.5 g
- Carbohydrates 4.5 g
- Sugar 0.5 g
- Protein 25.1 g
- Cholesterol 255 mg

Sweet Dijon Salmon

Preparation Time: 10 minutes
Cooking Time: 12 minutes
Serve: 4

Ingredients:

- 4 salmon fillets
- 2 tbsp olive oil
- 1 tsp garlic, minced
- 4 tbsp maple syrup
- ¼ cup Dijon mustard

Directions:

1. Preheat the oven to 400 F.
2. In a small bowl, mix oil, garlic, maple syrup, and Dijon mustard.
3. Brush salmon fillets with oil mixture and place onto the baking pan.
4. Bake for 12 minutes.
5. Serve and enjoy.

Nutritional Value (Amount per Serving):

- Calories 361
- Fat 18 g
- Carbohydrates 15 g
- Sugar 12 g
- Protein 34 g
- Cholesterol 75 mg

Flavorful Shrimp Fajitas

Preparation Time: 10 minutes

Cooking Time: 15 minutes

Serve: 4

Ingredients:

- 1 lb shrimp, peeled & deveined
- 2 tbsp olive oil
- 1 tbsp taco seasoning
- ½ lemon juice
- 1 onion, sliced
- 1 red bell pepper, sliced
- 2 yellow bell pepper, sliced

Directions:

1. Preheat the oven to 400 F.
2. Add shrimp and remaining ingredients into the mixing bowl and mix well.
3. Pour shrimp mixture into the baking pan.
4. Place the baking pan onto the oven rack and bake for 15 minutes.
5. Serve and enjoy.

Nutritional Value (Amount per Serving):

- Calories 230
- Fat 8 g
- Carbohydrates 12 g
- Sugar 5 g
- Protein 25 g
- Cholesterol 240 mg

Delicious Pesto Salmon

Preparation Time: 10 minutes
Cooking Time: 20 minutes
Serve: 4

Ingredients:

- 4 salmon fillets
- 1 onion, sliced
- 2 cups cherry tomatoes, cut in half
- ½ cup feta cheese, crumbled
- ½ cup basil pesto
- Pepper
- Salt

Directions:

1. Preheat the oven to 350 F.
2. Season salmon fillets with pepper and salt and place into the baking dish.
3. Pour remaining ingredients over salmon fillets.
4. Bake for 20 minutes.
5. Serve and enjoy.

Nutritional Value (Amount per Serving):

- Calories 445
- Fat 28 g
- Carbohydrates 8 g
- Sugar 6 g
- Protein 40 g
- Cholesterol 102 mg

Garlic Tilapia

Preparation Time: 10 minutes

Cooking Time: 15 minutes

Serve: 4

Ingredients:

- 1 lb tilapia fillets
- 2 tbsp olive oil
- 5 garlic cloves, minced
- Pepper
- Salt

Directions:

1. Preheat the oven to 400 F.
2. Season fish fillets with pepper and salt and place into the baking dish.
3. Mix oil and garlic and pour over fish fillets.
4. Place a baking dish onto the oven rack and bake for 15 minutes.
5. Serve and enjoy.

Nutritional Value (Amount per Serving):

- Calories 161
- Fat 8 g
- Carbohydrates 1 g
- Sugar 0.1 g
- Protein 20 g
- Cholesterol 55 mg

Flavors Catfish Fillets

Preparation Time: 10 minutes
Cooking Time: 15 minutes
Serve: 4

Ingredients:

- 1 lb catfish fillets
- 1 tbsp dried oregano, crushed
- 1 ½ tsp onion powder
- 1 tsp red chili flakes
- ½ tsp chili powder
- ½ tsp ground cumin
- Pepper
- Salt

Directions:

1. Preheat the oven to 350 F.
2. In a small bowl, mix cumin, chili powder, red chili flakes, onion powder, oregano, pepper, and salt and rub over fish fillets.
3. Place fish fillets into the baking dish.
4. Place a baking dish onto the oven rack and bake for 15 minutes.
5. Serve and enjoy.

Nutritional Value (Amount per Serving):

- Calories 166
- Fat 9 g
- Carbohydrates 2 g
- Sugar 0.5 g
- Protein 19 g
- Cholesterol 55 mg

Blackened Fish Fillets

Preparation Time: 10 minutes
Cooking Time: 12 minutes
Serve: 4

Ingredients:

- 4 mahi-mahi fillets
- ½ tsp onion powder
- 1 tsp ground cumin
- 1 tsp dried oregano
- ½ tsp cayenne
- 3 tbsp olive oil
- 1 tsp garlic powder
- 1 tsp smoked paprika
- ½ tsp pepper
- ½ tsp salt

Directions:

1. Preheat the oven to 400 F.
2. In a small bowl, mix onion powder, cumin, oregano, cayenne, garlic powder, paprika, pepper, and salt.
3. Brush fish fillets with oil and rub with spice mixture.
4. Place fish fillets into the baking dish.
5. Place baking dish onto the oven rack and bake for 12 minutes.
6. Serve and enjoy.

Nutritional Value (Amount per Serving):

- Calories 190
- Fat 12 g
- Carbohydrates 2 g
- Sugar 0.5 g
- Protein 20 g
- Cholesterol 85 mg

CHAPTER 6: VEGETABLES & SIDE DISHES

Parmesan Cauliflower Florets

Preparation Time: 10 minutes

Cooking Time: 30 minutes

Serve: 6

Ingredients:

- 1 medium cauliflower head, cut into florets
- ½ cup parmesan cheese, grated
- 1 cup breadcrumbs
- 1 tsp garlic, minced
- ½ cup butter, melted
- ¼ tsp pepper
- ¼ tsp salt

Directions:

1. Preheat the oven to 400 F.
2. In a small bowl, mix melted butter and garlic.
3. In a shallow dish, mix parmesan cheese, breadcrumbs, pepper, and salt.
4. Dip each cauliflower floret into the melted butter and coat with parmesan cheese mixture and place onto the parchment-lined baking pan.
5. Bake in preheated oven for 30 minutes.
6. Serve and enjoy.

Nutritional Value (Amount per Serving):

- Calories 280
- Fat 19.6 g
- Carbohydrates 18.3 g
- Sugar 3.4 g
- Protein 9.8 g
- Cholesterol 51 mg

Zucchini Tomato Bake

Preparation Time: 10 minutes
Cooking Time: 30 minutes
Serve: 6

Ingredients:

- 2 medium zucchini, sliced
- 5 medium tomatoes, sliced
- 2 medium yellow squash, sliced
- ½ tsp Italian seasoning
- ½ tsp onion powder
- ½ tsp garlic powder
- ½ cup parmesan cheese, shredded
- ½ tsp pepper

Directions:

1. Preheat the oven to 375 F.
2. In a greased baking dish, arrange zucchini, tomatoes, and squash in an alternating pattern.
3. Top with spices and cheese.
4. Bake for 25-30 minutes.
5. Serve and enjoy.

Nutritional Value (Amount per Serving):

- Calories 60
- Fat 2.3 g
- Carbohydrates 7 g
- Sugar 4 g
- Protein 4.4 g
- Cholesterol 5 mg

Zucchini Potato Gratin

Preparation Time: 10 minutes

Cooking Time: 50 minutes

Serve: 6

Ingredients:

- 1 ½ zucchini, cut into ¼-inch slices
- 5 small potatoes, cut into 1/8-inch slices
- 1 cup Gruyere cheese, grated
- 1 cup half and half
- 1 tsp herb de Provence
- 1 tsp garlic, minced
- ¼ tsp pepper
- 1 ¾ tsp salt

Directions:

1. Preheat the oven to 400 F.
2. Arrange vegetables in a circular pattern in a greased 8*6-inch baking dish
3. Mix half and half, herb de Provence, garlic, pepper, and salt and pour over vegetables.
4. Sprinkle grated cheese on top.
5. Bake for 50 minutes.
6. Serve and enjoy.

Nutritional Value (Amount per Serving):

- Calories 256
- Fat 6 g
- Carbohydrates 31 g
- Sugar 2 g
- Protein 10 g
- Cholesterol 35 mg

Spinach Zucchini Casserole

Preparation Time: 10 minutes
Cooking Time: 40 minutes
Serve: 6

Ingredients:

- 2 egg whites
- 3 cups baby spinach
- 2 small zucchini, diced
- ¼ cup parmesan cheese, grated
- 2 tsp garlic powder
- 1 tsp dried basil
- ½ cup breadcrumbs
- 2 small yellow squash, diced
- ¼ cup feta cheese, crumbled
- 1 tbsp olive oil
- ½ tsp pepper
- ½ tsp kosher salt

Directions:

1. Preheat the oven to 400 F.
2. Spray 9*13-inch casserole dish with cooking spray and set aside.
3. Heat oil in a pan over medium heat. Add squash, spinach, and zucchini into the pan and sauté for 5 minutes. Drain excess liquid and transfer vegetables into the mixing bowl.
4. Add remaining ingredients into the mixing bowl and mix well.
5. Pour mixture into the prepared casserole dish.
6. Place the casserole dish onto the oven rack and bake for 40 minutes.
7. Serve and enjoy.

Nutritional Value (Amount per Serving):

- Calories 102
- Fat 3.6 g
- Carbohydrates 10.8 g
- Sugar 2.6 g
- Protein 6.9 g
- Cholesterol 11 mg

Healthy Carrot Fries

Preparation Time: 10 minutes

Cooking Time: 25 minutes

Serve: 4

Ingredients:

- 4 medium carrots, peel & cut into fries shape
- 1 tsp ground cumin
- ½ tbsp smoked paprika
- 1 ½ tbsp olive oil
- ½ tsp salt

Directions:

1. Preheat the oven to 450 F.
2. Toss carrot fries with cumin, paprika, oil, and salt.
3. Arrange carrot fries onto the baking sheet and bake for 15 minutes.
4. Flip fries and bake for 10 minutes more.
5. Serve and enjoy.

Nutritional Value (Amount per Serving):

- Calories 85
- Fat 6 g
- Carbohydrates 7 g
- Sugar 3 g
- Protein 1 g
- Cholesterol 0 mg

Baked Curried Cauliflower Florets

Preparation Time: 10 minutes

Cooking Time: 15 minutes

Serve: 4

Ingredients:

- 2 lbs cauliflower, cut into florets
- 2 tsp fresh lemon juice
- 1 1/2 tsp curry powder
- 1 tbsp olive oil
- 1 tsp kosher salt

Directions:

1. Preheat the oven to 425 F.
2. Toss cauliflower florets with curry powder, oil, and salt.
3. Spread cauliflower florets onto the baking sheet and bake for 15 minutes.
4. Drizzle with lemon juice and serve.

Nutritional Value (Amount per Serving):

- Calories 90
- Fat 4 g
- Carbohydrates 12 g
- Sugar 5 g
- Protein 4 g
- Cholesterol 0 mg

Balsamic Mushrooms

Preparation Time: 10 minutes
Cooking Time: 20 minutes
Serve: 6

Ingredients:

* 1 lb button mushrooms, scrubbed
* 1/2 tsp dried oregano
* 1 tbsp garlic, crushed
* 2 tbsp olive oil
* 4 tbsp balsamic vinegar
* 1/2 tsp dried basil
* 1/4 tsp black pepper
* 1 tsp sea salt

Directions:

1. Preheat the oven to 425 F.
2. In a mixing bowl, add mushrooms and remaining ingredients and mix well and let it sit for 15 minutes.
3. Spread mushrooms onto the baking sheet and bake for 20 minutes.
4. Serve and enjoy.

Nutritional Value (Amount per Serving):

* Calories 60
* Fat 5 g
* Carbohydrates 3 g
* Sugar 1.5 g
* Protein 2.5 g
* Cholesterol 0 mg

Cheesy Broccoli Fritters

Preparation Time: 10 minutes

Cooking Time: 30 minutes

Serve: 4

Ingredients:

- 3 cups broccoli florets, cooked & chopped
- 2 garlic cloves, minced
- 2 eggs, lightly beaten
- ¼ cup breadcrumbs
- 2 cups cheddar cheese, shredded
- Pepper
- Salt

Directions:

1. Preheat the oven to 375 F.
2. Add all ingredients into the large bowl and mix until well combined.
3. Make equal shapes of patties from mixture and place onto the parchment-lined baking sheet and bake for 30 minutes. Flip patties halfway through.
4. Serve and enjoy.

Nutritional Value (Amount per Serving):

- Calories 295
- Fat 20 g
- Carbohydrates 6 g
- Sugar 1.7 g
- Protein 19.2 g
- Cholesterol 141 mg

Creamy Broccoli Casserole

Preparation Time: 10 minutes

Cooking Time: 30 minutes

Serve: 6

Ingredients:

- 15 oz frozen broccoli florets, defrosted and drained
- 1/3 cup milk
- 1/2 tsp onion powder
- 10.5 oz can cream of mushroom soup
- 1 cup cheddar cheese, shredded
- For topping:
- 1 tbsp butter, melted
- 1/2 cup cracker crumbs

Directions:

1. Preheat the oven to 350 F.
2. Add all ingredients except topping ingredients into the greased casserole dish.
3. In a small bowl, mix cracker crumbs and butter and sprinkle over dish mixture.
4. Place the casserole dish onto the oven rack and bake for 30 minutes.
5. Serve and enjoy.

Nutritional Value (Amount per Serving):

- Calories 192
- Fat 12.9 g
- Carbohydrates 10.5 g
- Sugar 2.4 g
- Protein 6.9 g
- Cholesterol 25 mg

Baked Sweet Potatoes & Apple

Preparation Time: 10 minutes
Cooking Time: 30 minutes
Serve: 2

Ingredients:

- 2 large green apples, diced
- 2 large sweet potatoes, diced
- 2 tbsp maple syrup
- 1 tbsp olive oil
- 2 tsp cinnamon

Directions:

1. Preheat the oven to 400 F.
2. In a mixing bowl, toss sweet potatoes, apples, cinnamon, and oil.
3. Spread sweet potatoes and apples onto the baking pan and bake in a preheated oven for 30 minutes.
4. Drizzle with maple syrup and serve.

Nutritional Value (Amount per Serving):

- Calories 350
- Fat 7 g
- Carbohydrates 75 g
- Sugar 35 g
- Protein 2 g
- Cholesterol 0 mg

CHAPTER 7: SNACKS & APPETIZERS

Bacon Jalapeno Poppers

Preparation Time: 10 minutes

Cooking Time: 30 minutes

Serve: 5

Ingredients:

- 10 jalapeno peppers, slice lengthwise & remove seeds
- 8 oz cream cheese
- 1 tbsp vinegar
- 1 cup bacon, cooked & chopped
- 1 cup green onion, chopped

Directions:

1. Preheat the oven to 375 F.
2. In a bowl, mix bacon, cream cheese, vinegar, and green onion.
3. Stuff bacon mixture into each jalapeno half.
4. Arrange stuffed jalapenos onto the parchment-lined baking pan and bake in a preheated oven for 30 minutes.
5. Serve and enjoy.

Nutritional Value (Amount per Serving):

- Calories 267
- Fat 24.8 g
- Carbohydrates 6.6 g
- Sugar 1.5 g
- Protein 7.3 g
- Cholesterol 50 mg

Perfect Crab Dip

Preparation Time: 10 minutes
Cooking Time: 20 minutes
Serve: 8

Ingredients:

- 1 lb crab meat
- ½ tsp pepper
- 1 ½ tbsp lemon juice
- 1 tbsp hot sauce
- 1 tbsp Worcestershire sauce
- 1 garlic clove, minced
- ¼ cup onion, minced
- 1 cup cheddar cheese, grated
- 1 cup pepper jack cheese, grated
- ¼ cup sour cream
- ¼ cup mayonnaise
- 8 oz cream cheese
- ½ tsp kosher salt

Directions:

1. Preheat the oven to 325 F.
2. In a bowl, beat sour cream, mayonnaise, and cream cheese until smooth.
3. Add remaining ingredients and mix until well combined.
4. Pour mixture into the baking dish and spread evenly.
5. Place a baking dish onto the oven rack and bake for 20 minutes.
6. Serve with crackers.

Nutritional Value (Amount per Serving):

- Calories 256
- Fat 19.6 g
- Carbohydrates 5 g
- Sugar 1.2 g
- Protein 13.2 g
- Cholesterol 81 mg

Yummy Corn Dip

Preparation Time: 10 minutes

Cooking Time: 20 minutes

Serve: 6

Ingredients:

- 15 oz can corn kernel, drained
- 1 tbsp green chilies, diced
- 2 green onions, sliced
- ½ bell pepper, diced
- ½ cup cheddar cheese, shredded
- 1 tsp smoked paprika
- ¼ cup sour cream
- 1/3 cup mayonnaise

Directions:

1. Preheat the oven to 350 F.
2. Add all ingredients into the mixing bowl and mix until well combined.
3. Pour mixture into the baking dish.
4. Place a baking dish onto the oven rack and bake for 20 minutes.
5. Serve with crackers.

Nutritional Value (Amount per Serving):

- Calories 174
- Fat 10.3 g
- Carbohydrates 18.6 g
- Sugar 3.9 g
- Protein 4.9 g
- Cholesterol 18 mg

Garlic Cheese Dip

Preparation Time: 10 minutes

Cooking Time: 20 minutes

Serve: 6

Ingredients:

- 2 cups ricotta cheese
- 1 tsp garlic, minced
- 1/2 cup mozzarella cheese, shredded
- 1 lemon zest
- 3 tbsp olive oil
- 1/4 cup parmesan cheese, shredded
- Pepper
- Salt

Directions:

1. Preheat the oven to 375 F.
2. Add all ingredients into the bowl and mix until well combined.
3. Pour mixture into the greased casserole dish.
4. Place the casserole dish onto the oven rack and bake for 20 minutes.
5. Serve and enjoy.

Nutritional Value (Amount per Serving):

- Calories 181
- Fat 14 g
- Carbohydrates 4.5 g
- Sugar 0.3 g
- Protein 10.1 g
- Cholesterol 27 mg

Baked Potato Wedges

Preparation Time: 10 minutes

Cooking Time: 15 minutes

Serve: 4

Ingredients:

- 2 potatoes, cut into wedges
- ½ tsp garlic powder
- ½ tsp paprika
- 1/8 tsp chili powder
- 2 tbsp olive oil
- Salt

Directions:

1. Preheat the oven to 350 F.
2. Soak potato wedges in the water for 1 hour. Drain well and pat dry with a paper towel.
3. In a bowl, toss potato wedges with oil, chili powder, paprika, garlic powder, and salt.
4. Spread potato wedges on the parchment-lined baking pan and bake for 15-20 minutes.
5. Serve and enjoy.

Nutritional Value (Amount per Serving):

- Calories 136
- Fat 7.2 g
- Carbohydrates 17.2 g
- Sugar 1.4 g
- Protein 1.9 g
- Cholesterol 0 mg

Healthy Vegetable Bites

Preparation Time: 10 minutes
Cooking Time: 20 minutes
Serve: 6

Ingredients:

- 1 egg
- 1 cup cooked quinoa
- 2 oz cheddar cheese, shredded
- 2 oz mozzarella cheese, shredded
- 1 cup mixed vegetables, cooked & chopped
- ½ tsp kosher salt

Directions:

1. Preheat the oven to 350 F.
2. Spray mini muffin tin with cooking spray and set aside.
3. Add all ingredients to a bowl and mix until well combined.
4. Divide the mixture between the cups of a prepared mini muffin tin, and press down.
5. Place muffin tin onto the oven rack and bake for 20 minutes.
6. Serve and enjoy.

Nutritional Value (Amount per Serving):

- Calories 194
- Fat 7.4 g
- Carbohydrates 21.6 g
- Sugar 0.1 g
- Protein 10.5 g
- Cholesterol 42 mg

Tasty Roasted Chickpeas

Preparation Time: 10 minutes

Cooking Time: 30 minutes

Serve: 4

Ingredients:

- 15 oz can chickpeas, drained & rinsed
- 1 tbsp olive oil
- 1 tsp chili powder
- ¼ tsp pepper
- 1 tsp salt

Directions:

1. Preheat the oven to 400 F.
2. Spread chickpeas onto the parchment-lined baking pan and bake for 15 minutes.
3. Remove chickpeas from the oven and place them into the bowl.
4. Add remaining ingredients to the bowl and toss well.
5. Bake chickpeas for 15 minutes more.
6. Serve and enjoy.

Nutritional Value (Amount per Serving):

- Calories 159
- Fat 4.8 g
- Carbohydrates 24.5 g
- Sugar 0.1 g
- Protein 5.4 g
- Cholesterol 0 mg

Cheesy Cauliflower Tots

Preparation Time: 10 minutes

Cooking Time: 25 minutes

Serve: 6

Ingredients:

- 1 egg
- 2 cups cauliflower florets
- 1/2 cup cheddar cheese, shredded
- 1/4 cup bell pepper, minced
- 1 small onion, minced
- 1/4 cup breadcrumbs
- 1/4 cup parmesan cheese, shredded
- Pepper
- Salt

Directions:

1. Preheat the oven to 375 F.
2. Boil cauliflower florets in hot water for 5 minutes.
3. Drain cauliflower and blend in a food processor.
4. Add blended cauliflower and remaining ingredients in bowl and mix until well combined.
5. Make small tots from cauliflower mixture and place onto the parchment-lined baking pan and bake in preheated oven for 20 minutes. Turn tots halfway through.
6. Serve and enjoy.

Nutritional Value (Amount per Serving):

- Calories 95
- Fat 5.1 g
- Carbohydrates 6.8 g
- Sugar 1.9 g
- Protein 6 g
- Cholesterol 40 mg

CHAPTER 8: DEHYDRATE

Yellow Squash Chips

Preparation Time: 10 minutes

Cooking Time: 5 hours

Serve: 4

Ingredients:

- 4 small yellow squash, cut into 1/8-inch slices
- 1 ½ tsp olive oil
- 1 ½ tsp sea salt

Directions:

1. In a bowl, toss squash slices with oil and salt.
2. Place rack onto a baking tray then arrange squash slices onto the rack. Insert into the oven.
3. Press dehydrate mode and set the timer to 5 hours.
4. Store squash chips in an air-tight container.

Nutritional Value (Amount per Serving):

- Calories 34
- Fat 2 g
- Carbohydrates 4 g
- Sugar 2 g
- Protein 1.4 g
- Cholesterol 0 mg

Eggplant Chips

Preparation Time: 10 minutes

Cooking Time: 5 hours

Serve: 6

Ingredients:

- 4 cups eggplant slices, sliced thinly
- ½ cup parmesan cheese, grated
- 1 tsp Italian seasoning
- ½ cup tomato sauce

Directions:

1. Brush eggplant slices with tomato sauce and sprinkle with parmesan cheese and Italian seasoning.
2. Place rack onto a baking tray then arrange eggplant slices onto the rack. Insert into the oven.
3. Press dehydrate mode and set the timer to 5 hours.
4. Store eggplant chips in an air-tight container.

Nutritional Value (Amount per Serving):

- Calories 121
- Fat 6.4 g
- Carbohydrates 4.4 g
- Sugar 2.6 g
- Protein 8.8 g
- Cholesterol 21 mg

Kiwi Chips

Preparation Time: 10 minutes

Cooking Time: 5 hours

Serve: 6

Ingredients:

- 6 kiwis, peel & cut into ¼-inch slices

Directions:

1. Place rack onto a baking tray then arrange kiwi slices onto the rack. Insert into the oven.
2. Press dehydrate mode and set the timer to 5 hours.
3. Store kiwi chips in an air-tight container.

Nutritional Value (Amount per Serving):

- Calories 46
- Fat 0.4 g
- Carbohydrates 11.1 g
- Sugar 6.8 g
- Protein 0.9 g
- Cholesterol 0 mg

Kale Chips

Preparation Time: 10 minutes

Cooking Time: 2 hours

Serve: 6

Ingredients:

- 3 bunches kale, remove stem & cut into bite-size pieces
- 1 tbsp olive oil
- 1 ½ tsp garlic powder
- 3 ½ tbsp nutritional yeast
- 1 tsp salt

Directions:

1. Add kale into the large bowl.
2. Add oil, garlic powder, and salt over the kale and mix well.
3. Sprinkle with nutritional yeast and toss well.
4. Place rack onto a baking tray then arrange kale pieces onto the rack. Insert into the oven.
5. Press dehydrate mode and set the timer to 2 hours.
6. Store kale chips in an air-tight container.

Nutritional Value (Amount per Serving):

- Calories 59
- Fat 2.7 g
- Carbohydrates 6.7 g
- Sugar 0.2 g
- Protein 3.8 g
- Cholesterol 0 mg

Zucchini Chips

Preparation Time: 10 minutes

Cooking Time: 5 hours

Serve: 4

Ingredients:

- 2 zucchini, sliced thinly
- ¼ tsp smoked paprika
- ¼ tsp chili powder
- Salt

Directions:

1. Add zucchini slices, smoked paprika, chili powder, and salt into the bowl and toss well.
2. Place rack onto a baking tray then arrange zucchini slices onto the rack. Insert into the oven.
3. Press dehydrate mode and set the timer to 5 hours.
4. Store zucchini chips in an air-tight container.

Nutritional Value (Amount per Serving):

- Calories 17
- Fat 0.2 g
- Carbohydrates 3.4 g
- Sugar 1.7 g
- Protein 1.2 g
- Cholesterol 0 mg

Banana Slices

Preparation Time: 10 minutes

Cooking Time: 5 hours

Serve: 4

Ingredients:

- 4 bananas, peel & cut into 1/8-inch slices

Directions:

1. Place rack onto a baking tray then arrange banana slices onto the rack. Insert into the oven.
2. Press dehydrate mode and set the timer to 5 hours.
3. Store banana slices in an air-tight container.

Nutritional Value (Amount per Serving):

- Calories 105
- Fat 0.4 g
- Carbohydrates 27 g
- Sugar 14.4 g
- Protein 1.3 g
- Cholesterol 0 mg

Pear Slices

Preparation Time: 10 minutes

Cooking Time: 5 hours

Serve: 4

Ingredients:

- 4 pears, cut into ¼-inch thick slices

Directions:

1. Place rack onto a baking tray then arrange pear slices onto the rack. Insert into the oven.
2. Press dehydrate mode and set the timer to 5 hours.
3. Store pear slices in an air-tight container.

Nutritional Value (Amount per Serving):

- Calories 121
- Fat 0.3 g
- Carbohydrates 31.8 g
- Sugar 20.4 g
- Protein 0.8 g
- Cholesterol 0 mg

Salmon Jerky

Preparation Time: 10 minutes

Cooking Time: 4 hours

Serve: 6

Ingredients:

- 1 lb salmon, cut into ¼-inch slices
- 6 tbsp soy sauce
- ¾ tbsp molasses
- 1 tbsp fresh lemon juice
- ½ tsp liquid smoke

Directions:

1.   Add salmon slices, soy sauce, liquid smoke, lemon juice, molasses, and soy sauce into the zip-lock bag, seal bag shake well and place in the refrigerator for overnight.

2.   Remove salmon slices from marinade.

3.   Place rack onto a baking tray then arrange salmon slices onto the rack. Insert into the oven.

4.   Press dehydrate mode and set the timer to 4 hours.

Nutritional Value (Amount per Serving):

- Calories 116
- Fat 4.7 g
- Carbohydrates 3.1 g
- Sugar 1.7 g
- Protein 15.7 g
- Cholesterol 33 mg

CHAPTER 9: DESSERTS

Delicious Pineapple Bars

Preparation Time: 10 minutes

Cooking Time: 35 minutes

Serve: 12

Ingredients:

* 2 eggs
* 1 ¼ cup crushed pineapple, drained
* ¼ tsp baking soda
* 1 cup all-purpose flour
* 1 cup sugar
* ½ cup butter, softened
* Pinch of salt

Directions:

1. Preheat the oven to 350 F.
2. Spray 9*9-inch baking pan with cooking spray and set aside.
3. In a mixing bowl, mix together eggs, sugar, and butter.
4. Add baking soda, flour, and salt and beat until well combined.
5. Add crushed pineapple and stir well.
6. Pour mixture into the prepared baking pan.
7. Place the baking pan onto the oven rack and bake for 35 minutes.
8. Remove from the oven and let it cool for 10 minutes.
9. Cut into pieces and serve.

Nutritional Value (Amount per Serving):

* Calories 187
* Fat 8.5 g
* Carbohydrates 27 g
* Sugar 18.5 g
* Protein 2.2 g
* Cholesterol 48 mg

Cinnamon Honey Pears

Preparation Time: 10 minutes

Cooking Time: 30 minutes

Serve: 4

Ingredients:

- 4 pears, peel, cut in half & scoop out & core
- ½ tsp vanilla
- ½ tsp ground cinnamon
- 2 tbsp butter, melted
- 3 tbsp honey

Directions:

1. Preheat the oven to 400 F.
2. Place pears in a 9*13-inch baking dish.
3. In a small bowl, mix honey, melted butter, cinnamon, and vanilla.
4. Pour honey mixture over pears.
5. Place baking dish onto the oven rack and bake for 30 minutes.
6. Remove from the oven and let it cool for 5-10 minutes.
7. Serve and enjoy.

Nutritional Value (Amount per Serving):

- Calories 222
- Fat 6.1 g
- Carbohydrates 45.1 g
- Sugar 33.4 g
- Protein 0.9 g
- Cholesterol 15 mg

Cinnamon Apple Slices

Preparation Time: 10 minutes

Cooking Time: 30 minutes

Serve: 4

Ingredients:

- 3 apples, cut into ½-inch thick wedges
- 1/3 cup butter, melted
- ½ tsp ground cinnamon
- 2 tbsp brown sugar

Directions:

1. Preheat the oven to 350 F.
2. Add apple slices into the large mixing bowl.
3. In a small bowl, mix brown sugar, melted butter, and cinnamon until sugar is dissolved.
4. Pour sugar mixture over apple slices and mix until well coated.
5. Pour apple slices into the baking dish.
6. Place baking dish onto the oven rack and bake for 30 minutes. Stir apple slices after every 10 minutes.
7. Serve baked apple slices with vanilla ice-cream.

Nutritional Value (Amount per Serving):

- Calories 240
- Fat 15.7 g
- Carbohydrates 27.8 g
- Sugar 21.8 g
- Protein 0.6 g
- Cholesterol 41 mg

Moist Yogurt Cake

Preparation Time: 10 minutes
Cooking Time: 40 minutes
Serve: 8

Ingredients:

- 2 eggs
- 2 cups all-purpose flour
- 1 cup plain yogurt
- 1 lemon zest
- ½ tsp vanilla
- 2 tsp baking powder
- ½ cup canola oil
- ½ cup sugar
- 3 tbsp orange jam
- Pinch of salt

Directions:

1. Preheat the oven to 350 F.
2. Grease 9.5*2.5-inch loaf pan and set aside.
3. Add eggs, yogurt, vanilla, lemon zest, oil, and sugar in mixing bowl and beat until smooth.
4. Add baking powder, flour, and salt and mix until just combined.
5. Pour batter into the prepared loaf pan.
6. Place loaf pan onto the oven rack and bake for 35-40 minutes.
7. Remove loaf pan from the oven and let it cool for 10 minutes.
8. Spread orange jam on top of the cake.
9. Slice and serve.

Nutritional Value (Amount per Serving):

- Calories 321
- Fat 15.4 g
- Carbohydrates 39.2 g
- Sugar 14.9 g
- Protein 6.4 g
- Cholesterol 43 mg

Easy Blonde Brownie

Preparation Time: 10 minutes
Cooking Time: 20 minutes
Serve: 8

Ingredients:

- 2 eggs
- ½ cup chocolate chips
- 2 cup all-purpose flour
- 2 tsp baking powder
- 1 ½ tsp vanilla
- 1 ¼ cup brown sugar
- 1 cup butter, melted
- ½ tsp salt

Directions:

1. Preheat the oven to 350 F.
2. Grease 9*13-inch baking pan and set aside.
3. In a mixing bowl, mix melted butter and sugar. Add vanilla and eggs and mix well.
4. Add flour, baking powder, and salt and mix until well combined.
5. Add chocolate chips and stir well.
6. Pour batter into the prepared pan and spread evenly.
7. Place the baking pan onto the oven rack and bake for 20 minutes.
8. Remove from the oven and let it cool completely.
9. Slice and serve.

Nutritional Value (Amount per Serving):

- Calories 479
- Fat 27.5 g
- Carbohydrates 53.1 g
- Sugar 27.7 g
- Protein 5.7 g
- Cholesterol 104 mg

Fudgy Chocolate Brownies

Preparation Time: 10 minutes
Cooking Time: 20 minutes
Serve: 16

Ingredients:

- 2 eggs
- ½ cup flour
- 1 tsp vanilla
- 1 cup sugar
- ½ cup cocoa powder
- ½ cup butter, melted
- ¼ tsp salt

Directions:

1. Preheat the oven to 350 F.
2. Grease 8*8-inch pan and set aside.
3. In a bowl, mix cocoa powder and melted butter. Add sugar and stir until dissolved.
4. Add vanilla and eggs and mix until well combined.
5. Add flour and salt and stir until combine.
6. Pour batter in prepared pan and spread evenly.
7. Place the pan onto the oven rack and bake for 20 minutes.
8. Remove from the oven and let it cool completely.
9. Slice and serve.

Nutritional Value (Amount per Serving):

- Calories 127
- Fat 6.7 g
- Carbohydrates 17 g
- Sugar 12.6 g
- Protein 1.6 g
- Cholesterol 36 mg

Soft & Moist Lemon Brownies

Preparation Time: 10 minutes

Cooking Time: 20 minutes

Serve: 16

Ingredients:

- 2 eggs
- ½ tsp baking powder
- ¾ cup all-purpose flour
- 1 tbsp fresh lemon juice
- ½ lemon zest
- ¾ cup sugar
- ½ cup butter, softened

Directions:

1. Preheat the oven to 350 F.
2. Grease 8*8-inch pan and set aside.
3. In a large bowl, beat sugar, butter, and lemon zest until fluffy.
4. Add eggs, lemon juice, and flour and mix until combined.
5. Pour batter into the prepared pan and spread evenly.
6. Place the pan onto the oven rack and bake for 20 minutes.
7. Remove from the oven and let it cool completely.
8. Slice and serve.

Nutritional Value (Amount per Serving):

- Calories 116
- Fat 6.4 g
- Carbohydrates 14 g
- Sugar 9.5 g
- Protein 1.4 g
- Cholesterol 36 mg

Easy Lemon Cookies

Preparation Time: 10 minutes
Cooking Time: 11 minutes
Serve: 12

Ingredients:

- 1 egg yolk
- ½ tsp baking powder
- ¼ tsp baking soda
- 1 lemon zest
- 2 tsp vanilla
- 1 tbsp brown sugar
- 1 cup sugar
- 1 ¼ cups flour
- ½ cup butter, softened
- ¼ tsp salt

Directions:

1. Preheat the oven to 350 F.
2. In a bowl, mix flour, baking powder, baking soda, and salt.
3. In a separate bowl, beat butter, ¾ cup sugar, and brown sugar until fluffy.
4. Add eggs, vanilla, and lemon zest and beat until just combined.
5. Slowly add flour mixture and mix until just combined.
6. Make 1 ½-inch ball from mixture and roll into the remaining sugar and place onto the parchment-lined baking pan.
7. Bake in preheated oven for 11 minutes.
8. Remove from the oven and let it cool completely.
9. Serve and enjoy.

Nutritional Value (Amount per Serving):

- Calories 187
- Fat 8.2 g
- Carbohydrates 27.6 g
- Sugar 17.6 g
- Protein 1.7 g
- Cholesterol 38 mg

Chocolate Chip Cookies

Preparation Time: 10 minutes
Cooking Time: 8 minutes
Serve: 30

Ingredients:

- 1 egg
- 12 oz chocolate chips
- 2 cups self-rising flour
- ½ cup brown sugar
- 2/3 cup sugar
- 1 tsp vanilla
- 1 cup butter, softened

Directions:

1. Preheat the oven to 375 F.
2. In a bowl, mix egg, vanilla, and butter.
3. Add brown sugar and sugar and beat until creamy.
4. Slowly add flour and mix until just combined.
5. Add chocolate chips and stir well.
6. Spoon out cookie dough onto the parchment-lined baking pan.
7. Bake in preheated oven for 8-10 minutes.
8. Remove from the oven and let it cool completely.
9. Serve and enjoy.

Nutritional Value (Amount per Serving):

- Calories 174
- Fat 9.7 g
- Carbohydrates 19.9 g
- Sugar 12.7 g
- Protein 2 g
- Cholesterol 24 mg

CHAPTER 10: 30-DAY MEAL PLAN

Day 1
Breakfast- Apple Oat Cups
Lunch-Spinach Zucchini Casserole
Dinner- Smoked Paprika Pork Chops

Day 2
Breakfast- Spinach Tomato Egg Muffins
Lunch-Zucchini Potato Gratin
Dinner-Beef Zucchini Burger Patties

Day 3
Breakfast- Perfect Potato Casserole
Lunch-Zucchini Tomato Bake
Dinner-Greek Lamb Patties

Day 4
Breakfast- Ham Cheese Casserole
Lunch-Blackened Fish Fillets
Dinner-Rosemary Pork Chops

Day 5
Breakfast- Fluffy Breakfast Egg Muffins
Lunch-Easy Brown Sugar Chicken
Dinner-Juicy Pork Tenderloin

Day 6
Breakfast- Pumpkin Bread
Lunch-Garlic Butter Shrimp
Dinner- Baked Pork Ribs

Day 7
Breakfast- Healthy Banana Bread
Lunch-Simple Cajun Salmon
Dinner- Rosemary Pork Chops

Day 8
Breakfast- Baked Oatmeal
Lunch-Creamy Chicken
Dinner-Baked Pork Patties

Day 9
Breakfast- Healthy Oat Muffins
Lunch-Delicious Turkey Cutlets
Dinner-Pork Chops with Potatoes

Day 10
Breakfast- Baked Cinnamon Oatmeal

Lunch-Sweet Dijon Salmon
Dinner-Quick Ranch Pork Chops

Day 11
Breakfast- Apple Oat Cups
Lunch-Flavorful Shrimp Fajitas
Dinner- Simple Spiced Pork Chops

Day 12
Breakfast- Spinach Tomato Egg Muffins
Lunch-Flavors Catfish Fillets
Dinner-Beef Onion Bake

Day 13
Breakfast- Perfect Potato Casserole
Lunch-Delicious Pesto Salmon
Dinner- Pork Chops with Potatoes

Day 14
Breakfast- Ham Cheese Casserole
Lunch-Turkey Spinach Patties
Dinner- Rosemary Pork Chops

Day 15
Breakfast- Fluffy Breakfast Egg Muffins
Lunch-Juicy Chicken Drumsticks
Dinner- Beef Zucchini Burger Patties

Day 16
Breakfast- Apple Oat Cups
Lunch-Spinach Zucchini Casserole
Dinner- Smoked Paprika Pork Chops

Day 17
Breakfast- Spinach Tomato Egg Muffins
Lunch-Zucchini Potato Gratin
Dinner-Beef Zucchini Burger Patties

Day 18
Breakfast- Perfect Potato Casserole
Lunch-Zucchini Tomato Bake
Dinner-Greek Lamb Patties

Day 19
Breakfast- Ham Cheese Casserole
Lunch-Blackened Fish Fillets
Dinner-Rosemary Pork Chops

Day 20
Breakfast- Fluffy Breakfast Egg Muffins
Lunch-Easy Brown Sugar Chicken
Dinner-Juicy Pork Tenderloin
Day 21
Breakfast- Pumpkin Bread
Lunch-Garlic Butter Shrimp
Dinner- Baked Pork Ribs
Day 22
Breakfast- Healthy Banana Bread
Lunch-Simple Cajun Salmon
Dinner- Rosemary Pork Chops
Day 23
Breakfast- Baked Oatmeal
Lunch-Creamy Chicken
Dinner-Baked Pork Patties
Day 24
Breakfast- Healthy Oat Muffins
Lunch-Delicious Turkey Cutlets
Dinner-Pork Chops with Potatoes
Day 25
Breakfast- Baked Cinnamon Oatmeal

Lunch-Sweet Dijon Salmon
Dinner-Quick Ranch Pork Chops
Day 26
Breakfast- Apple Oat Cups
Lunch-Flavorful Shrimp Fajitas
Dinner- Simple Spiced Pork Chops
Day 27
Breakfast- Spinach Tomato Egg Muffins
Lunch-Flavors Catfish Fillets
Dinner-Beef Onion Bake
Day 28
Breakfast- Perfect Potato Casserole
Lunch-Delicious Pesto Salmon
Dinner- Pork Chops with Potatoes
Day 29
Breakfast- Ham Cheese Casserole
Lunch-Turkey Spinach Patties
Dinner- Rosemary Pork Chops
Day 30
Breakfast- Fluffy Breakfast Egg Muffins
Lunch-Juicy Chicken Drumsticks
Dinner- Beef Zucchini Burger Patties

APPENDIX : RECIPES INDEX

A

Advantages of Oven 8
Apple Oat Cups 10

B

Bacon Jalapeno Poppers 65
Baked Cinnamon Oatmeal 19
Baked Curried Cauliflower Florets 60
Baked Oatmeal 17
Baked Pork Patties 34
Baked Pork Ribs 37
Baked Potato Wedges 69
Baked Salmon Patties 45
Baked Sweet Potatoes & Apple 64
Balsamic Mushrooms 61
Banana Slices 78
Beef Onion Bake 30
Beef Zucchini Burger Patties 43
Blackened Fish Fillets 54

C

Cheesy Broccoli Fritters 62
Cheesy Cauliflower Tots 72
Chicken Meatballs 29
Chocolate Chip Cookies 89
Cinnamon Apple Slices 83
Cinnamon Honey Pears 82
Control Buttons and Functions 7
Creamy Broccoli Casserole 63
Creamy Chicken 27
Crispy Chicken Wings 21

D

Delicious Pesto Salmon 51
Delicious Pineapple Bars 81
Delicious Turkey Cutlets 23

E

Easy Blonde Brownie 85
Easy Brown Sugar Chicken 28
Easy Lemon Cookies 88
Eggplant Chips 74

F

Features of Oven 6
Flavorful Shrimp Fajitas 50
Flavors Catfish Fillets 53
Fluffy Breakfast Egg Muffins 14
Fudgy Chocolate Brownies 86

G

Garlic Butter Shrimp 48
Garlic Cheese Dip 68
Garlic Tilapia 52
Greek Lamb Patties 40

H

Ham Cheese Casserole 13
Healthy Banana Bread 16
Healthy Carrot Fries 59
Healthy Chicken Fritters 26
Healthy Oat Muffins 18
Healthy Vegetable Bites 70

J

Juicy Chicken Drumsticks 20
Juicy Pork Tenderloin 38

K

Kale Chips 76
Kiwi Chips 75

L

Lamb Meatballs 41
Lemon Pepper Chicken Wings 22

M

Meatballs 35
Moist Yogurt Cake 84

O

Oster Digital French Door Oven 6

P

Parmesan Cauliflower Florets 55
Pear Slices 79
Perfect Crab Dip 66
Perfect Potato Casserole 12
Pork Chops with Potatoes 33
Pork Meatballs 42
Pumpkin Bread 15

Q

Quick Ranch Pork Chops 32

R

Rosemary Pork Chops 39

S

Salmon Jerky 80
Simple Cajun Salmon 46
Simple Lamb Patties 36
Simple Spiced Pork Chops 31
Smoked Paprika Pork Chops 44
Soft & Moist Lemon Brownies 87
Spinach Tomato Egg Muffins 11
Spinach Zucchini Casserole 58
Sweet Dijon Salmon 49

T

Tasty Crab Patties 47
Tasty Roasted Chickpeas 71
Turkey Meatballs 25
Turkey Spinach Patties 24

Y

Yellow Squash Chips 73
Yummy Corn Dip 67

Z

Zucchini Chips 77
Zucchini Potato Gratin 57
Zucchini Tomato Bake 56

CPSIA information can be obtained
at www.ICGtesting.com
Printed in the USA
BVHW011500111121
621204BV00005B/236